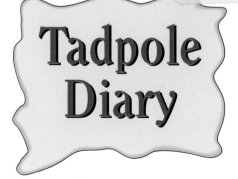

Tadpole Diary

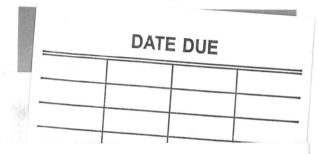

DATE DUE

Contents

How do tadpoles grow and
change into frogs?

Our class decided to find out
by watching some tadpoles and
writing down what we saw.

We called our book
Tadpole Diary.

Week 1

We found some frogs' eggs in a pond and brought them home. The eggs were soft like jelly and we could see inside them.

What's in the picture?

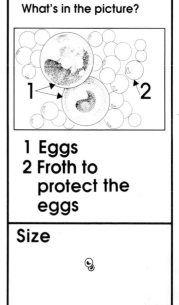

1 Eggs
2 Froth to protect the eggs

Size

4

Diary: Inside the eggs

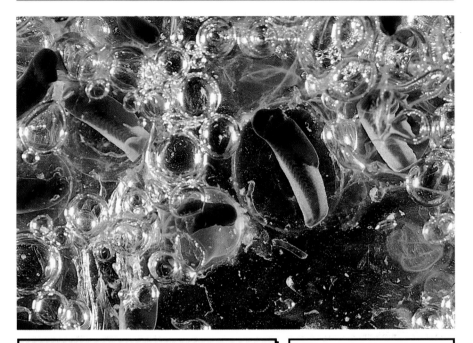

<table>
<tr><td>Week
1</td><td>Inside each egg was a tiny tadpole. You could see it under a magnifying glass. We're going to keep them in a fish tank near the window to see if they hatch.</td></tr>
</table>

What's in the picture?

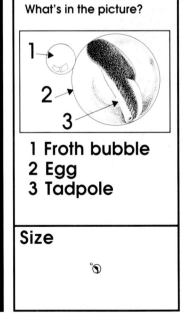

1 Froth bubble
2 Egg
3 Tadpole

Size

5

Diary: The tadpoles hatch

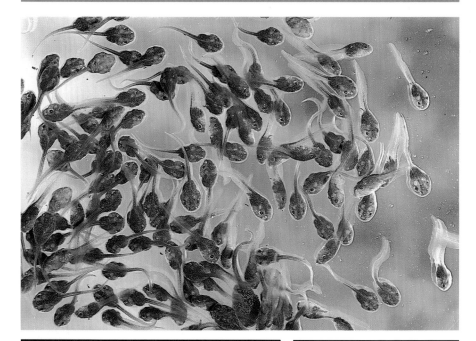

Some of the tadpoles have hatched! More tadpoles hatch each day. None of them have legs yet, but they can move by wriggling their tails. They always stay together.

What's in the picture?

1 Supporting rod
2 Eye

Size

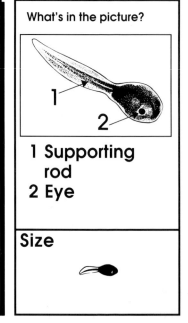

6

Week 4 Tadpoles breathe under water. They breathe through a little hole called a spiracle. We found the hole on the left side of its body. At first we thought it was its ear.

What's in the picture?

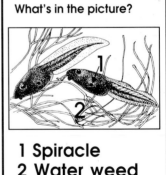

1 Spiracle
2 Water weed

Size

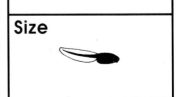

7

Diary: The back legs

Week 9 Some of our tadpoles have started to grow their back legs. But their bodies seem to have stopped growing. Why is this? We decided to look it up in a tadpole book.

What's in the picture?

1 Back leg
2 Soft papilla used to find food

Size

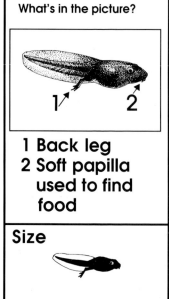

Diary: The front legs

Week 12 We found a book about tadpoles. It said tadpoles grow faster if you keep the water warm. Now they are growing their front legs. Sometimes they come up to swallow some air.

What's in the picture?

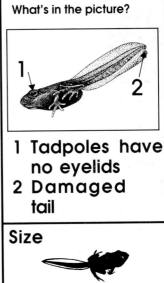

1 Tadpoles have no eyelids
2 Damaged tail

Size

9

Diary: Froglets have tails

Week 15 Today our first froglet came out of the water. It climbed up a stick that we'd put in the fish tank. The froglet looked like a frog, but it still had its tail.
We called him Fred.

What's in the picture?

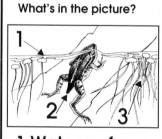

1 Water surface
2 Tail
3 Water weed

Size

10

Diary: The tail disappears

Week **16**	Soon afterward we saw his tail shrink. Fred had

become a frog. We took him back to the place where we found the eggs, and we let our frog go.
Goodbye, Fred!

What's in the picture?

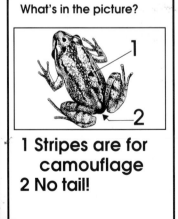

1 Stripes are for camouflage
2 No tail!

Size

Where can you find tadpoles?

In ponds and pools, wherever there is fresh, still water. Even in puddles beside the road sometimes.

What do tadpoles eat?

Stage	Food
in the egg	egg yolk
just hatched	egg yolk
young tadpole	water weed
older tadpole	water weed, tiny animals in the water, sometimes other tadpoles

Tadpole facts

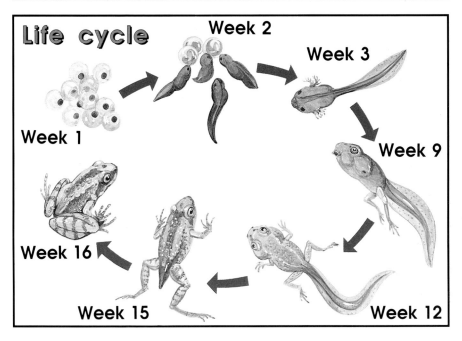

Life cycle

Week 1

Week 2

Week 3

Week 9

Week 12

Week 15

Week 16

Do all tadpoles turn into frogs?

All tadpoles become either frogs or toads, unless they are eaten first. Every tadpole goes through the stages shown in the diagram.

Does the tadpole in this book have a name?

Yes. The tadpole described in this book is called Limnodynastes (say "Lim-no-die-NAS-tees").

13

Frog facts

How many kinds are there?

There are more than 3000 different kinds of frog in the world.

Every year another 100 kinds of frog are discovered.

What do frogs eat?

Live insects, spiders, worms and grubs. Some big frogs eat mice.

Why do frogs have sticky tongues?

Frogs flip out their tongues to catch flying insects. The insects stick to the tongue.

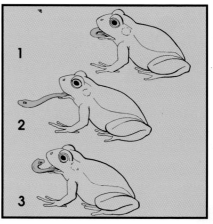

Frog facts

Why do frogs have long legs?

Frogs use their long back legs to jump high in the air, so they can catch flying insects.

How long do frogs live?

Most frogs live for three to five years.

Keeping tadpoles

Why not keep your
own tadpoles?
Follow these steps.

1 Collect frogs' eggs
with the water you
found them in.

2 Put them in a fish
bowl.
Change the
water every 2 days.

3 Feed them boiled
lettuce each day.

4 Put a stick in the
water so the froglets
can climb out.

5 Take the young frogs
back to the pond.
They can't survive
at home.